Welcome to the World of Giggles and Grins!

Hey there, amazing reader!

Are you ready to embark on a laughter-filled adventure? If you love giggles, chuckles, and belly laughs, then you're in the right place! This book is like a magical treasure chest, overflowing with jokes, funny stories, and hilarious surprises that will keep you laughing from start to finish.

Imagine a place where elephants paint rainbows, where dogs solve mysteries, and where bananas go to the doctor just because they're not peeling well! A place where every page is a new opportunity to laugh, smile, and let your imagination run wild.

As you turn these pages, remember: laughter is like a superpower. It can make a cloudy day sunny, turn a frown upside down, and make you feel like you can fly! So, get ready to unleash your superpower, giggle with every word, and let your heart be light and merry.

Invite your friends, your family, or your favorite stuffed animals to join you on this joyous journey. Share the jokes, tell the tales, and spread the happiness. Because when it comes to laughter, the more the merrier!

Remember laughter is most effective used at appropriate moments and fully enjoyed. Watch out for telling too many jokes and losing the impact.

So, take a deep breath, open to the first page, and dive into a world where the only rule is to laugh out loud, as loud as you can! Let's make this journey the funniest adventure ever!

Are you ready? Set? Let's go! 🚀🤣📚

Why did the bicycle fall
over?

Because it was two-tired!

What Do You Call a
Sleeping Bull?
A Bulldozer!

What's a Vampire's Favorite Fruit?

A Blood Orange!

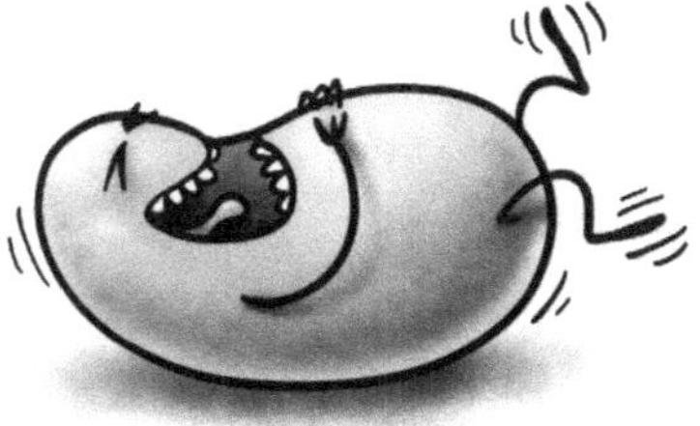

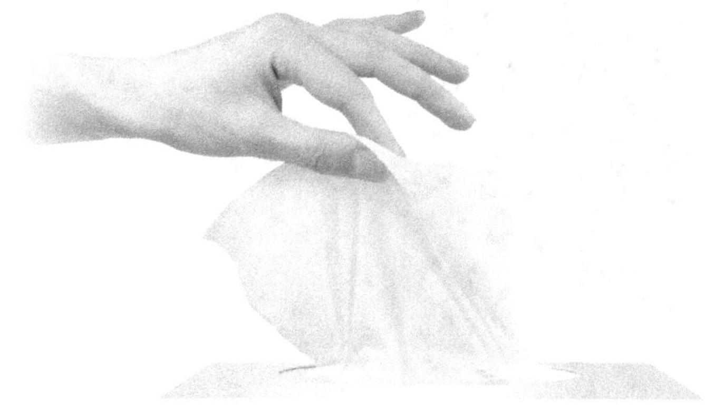

How do you make a Tissue
Dance?

Put a little boogie in it!

What do you call a bear
with no teeth?

A gummy bear!

Why was the computer
cold?

It left Its windows open!

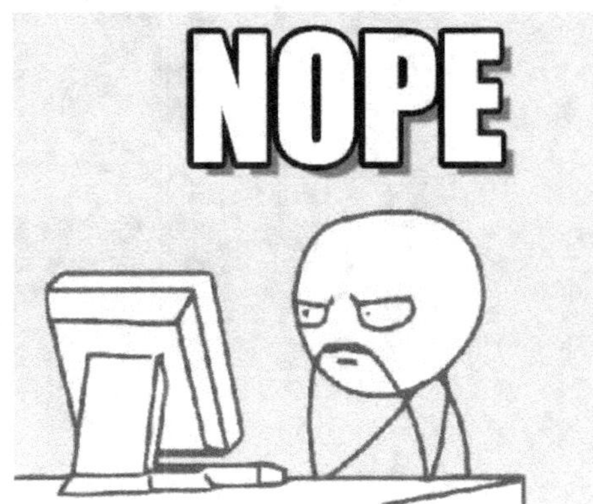

What do you call cheese
that's not yours?
Nacho Cheese!
NOPE

MATHEMATICS 10
(Science Group)

Why does the math book
look so sad?

Because it had too
many Problems!

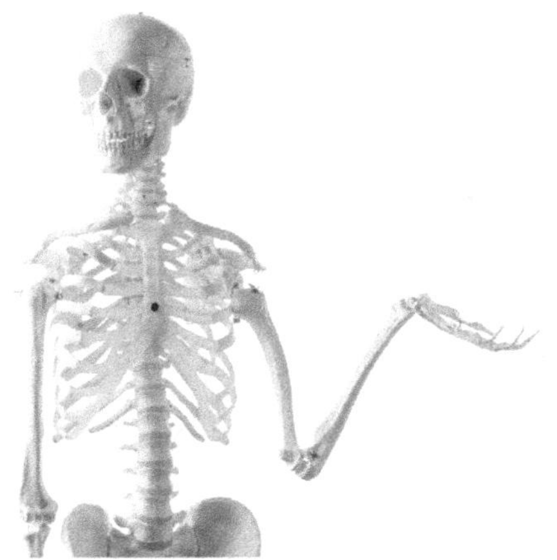
Why don't skeletons fight
each other?
They don't have the
guts!

Why did the scarecrow win an award?
Because he was outstanding in his field!

What do you call a fake Noddle?
An Impasta!

What happens when the
frog parks illegally?

It gets Toad!

Why did the golfer bring two pairs of pants?
In case he gets a hole in one!

LOL!

Why don't eggs tell jokes?
They'd crack each other up!

What did the Janitor say when he jumped out of the closet?

Supplies!

Why couldn't the Leopard play hide and seek?
Because he was always spotted!

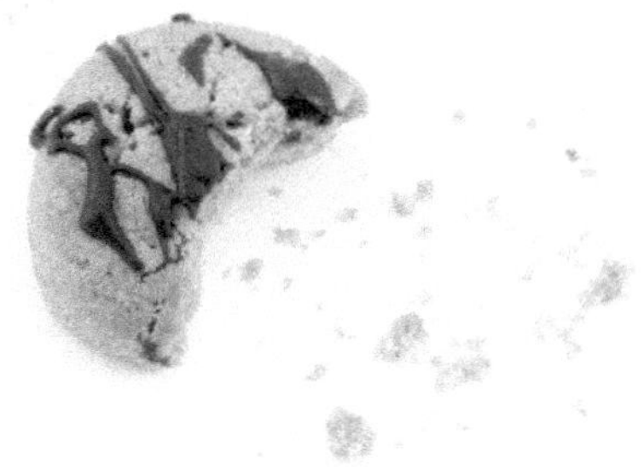

Why did the cookie go see
the doctor?

Because it felt crummy!

What's a ghost's favorite fruit?
A Boo-berry!

Story Time

Once there was a magician who was really bad at his job. He tried to pull a rabbit out of his hat but instead pulled out a cake. Everyone was shocked, but the magician said, "Don't worry, it's just a piece of cake!"

A bunny loved to bake, but everything turned out carrot-flavored. One day, it made a carrot cake that tasted like chocolate. Surprised, the bunny said, "Looks like I've got a new trick up my sleeve, or should I say, in my cake!"

A caterpillar was worried about growing up. It asked a butterfly, "What will I be when I grow up?" The butterfly said, "You'll still be you, just with better wings!"

An astronaut went to space but forgot something important. He called mission control, "I've forgotten my sandwich!" Mission control replied, "No worries, you'll just have to *launch* later!"

What's the cat's favorite color?
Purr-ple!

What do you call a dinosaur who is a noisy sleeper?

A bronto-snorus!

What do you get when you cross a snowman and a vampire?
Frostbite!

What do you call an ant
who fights crime?

A vigil-anty!

What did the ocean say to
the other ocean?

Nothing, they just
waved!

Knock knock.
Who's there?
Interrupting cow.
Interrupting c-
Moo!!!

Knock knock.

Who's there?

Banana.

Banana who?

Banana phone!

Banana Phone?

Ring Ring, banana phone!

Knock knock.
Who's there?
Boo.
Boo who?
Don't cry, it's just a joke!

Knock knock.

Who's there?

Lettuce.

Lettuce who?

Lettuce in, it's too cold out here!

Knock knock.
Who's there?
Cow says.
Cow says who?
No, silly, Cow says Moo!

Knock knock.

Who's there?

Atch.

Atch who?

Bless you! need a tissue?

Knock knock.

Who's there?

Dishes.

Dishes who?

Dishes a very bad joke!

Knock knock.
Who's there?
Bacon.
Bacon who?
Bacon a cake for your birthday!

Knock knock.
Who's there?
Bus.
Bus who?
Bus be friends, you're really cool!

Knock knock.
Who's there?
Bear.
Bear who?
Bear with me I got more jokes!

Knock knock.
Who's there?
Art.
Art who?
Art you glad you brought your crayons today?

In the Smith family kitchen, Dad decided to be a chef for a day. He twirled spaghetti like a cowboy's lasso, but oops! The spaghetti landed on the ceiling, looking like wiggly worms! The family couldn't stop giggling, especially when their cat, Whiskers, tried jumping to catch the dangling noodles.

Mrs. Johnson woke up and declared it was Backwards Day. She wore her shirt inside out, read books from back to front, and even walked backwards! Her kids laughed till their bellies ached, especially when Mom tried to make a sandwich and put the bread in the middle!

Mr. Carter Challenged his kids to a dance-off. He did the robot, the moonwalk, and even tried breakdancing! His moves were so funny and wobbly, the neighbors' dog started howling along, thinking it was a new game!

What's the best thing about Switzerland?.
I don't know, but the flag is a big plus!

The Grand Finale of Giggles!

Dear Superstar of Smiles,

As we come to the end of this laughter-packed adventure, I want to say a huge THANK YOU! Thank you for being the amazing, shining star that you are. Your love for humor and your eagerness to share joy with others is truly special.

Remember, every time you tell a joke, you're not just making people laugh – you're creating happiness, spreading cheer, and lighting up the room like a bright, beautiful star. Your sense of humor is a gift, and when you share it, you make the world a better, brighter, and much more fun place!

You've learned so many jokes, giggled at so many funny stories, and now, you're ready to spread laughter everywhere you go. Your parents, friends, and everyone you meet are so lucky to have a fantastic jokester like you in their lives.

Keep telling those jokes, keep practicing your punchlines, and most importantly, keep being your wonderful, unique self. You have a superpower – the power to make people happy – and that's the best superpower of all!

So, go ahead, Superstar, take your laughter, your joy, and your fantastic jokes into the world. Make it laugh, make it smile, and remember, you are absolutely incredible!

Until our next laughter adventure, keep giggling, keep joking, and keep being the amazing you!

With a big smile and a final chuckle,

[Your Joke Book]